BUILD YOUR BUSINESS

START YOUR YARD-WORK BUSINESS

by Amie Jane Leavitt

CAPSTONE PRESS
a capstone imprint

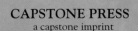

Snap Books are published by Capstone Press
1710 Roe Crest Drive, North Mankato, Minnesota 56003
www.mycapstone.com

Library of Congress Cataloging-in-Publication Data
Names: Leavitt, Amie Jane, author.
Title: Start your yard-work business / by Amie Jane Leavitt.
Description: North Mankato, Minnesota : Capstone Press, [2017] | Series: Snap books. Build your business | Audience: Ages 8–14. | Audience: Grades 4 to 6. | Includes bibliographical references and index.
Identifiers: LCCN 2016047900| ISBN 9781515766926 (library binding) | ISBN 9781515767046 (ebook (pdf)
Subjects: LCSH: Lawn care industry—Juvenile literature. | Lawns—Juvenile literature. | Money-making projects for children—Juvenile literature. | New business enterprises—Juvenile literature. | Entrepreneurship—Juvenile literature.
Classification: LCC SB433.27 .L43 2017 | DDC 635.9/647—dc23
LC record available at https://lccn.loc.gov/2016047900

EDITORIAL CREDITS

Editor: Gena Chester
Designer: Veronica Scott
Media Researcher: Kelly Garvin
Production Specialist: Laura Manthe

PHOTO CREDITS

Alamy: Alamy Stock Photo/Blend Images, 12, Selwyn, 9 (bottom), Jim West, 7; Getty Images/Jon Riley, 5; iStockphoto: asiseeit, 17, Michael Courtney, 16; Shutterstock: Ahlapot, 21, Andrey Burmakin, 20, Arman Zhenikeyev, 14, Barabasa, 15 (left), bikeriderlondon, 6, Billion Photos, 24 (t), Blend Images, 28-29, Casper1774 Studio, 23, docent, cover, Hurst Photo, cover, Jillian Cain Photography, 26-27, Koliadznska Iryna, 18, kryzhov, 19, lightpoet, 25, Ljupco Smokovski, 27 (t), MBLifestyle, 15 (top right), Mark Herreid, 15 (bottom right), nexus 7, 2, 30, 32, Nikola Bilic, 3, 31, OlegDoroshin, 13 (b), photka, 1, ShaunWilkinson, 13 (t), travis manley, 8, Uber Images, 10, Vitalliy, 24 (b), WilleeCole Photography, 22

Artistic elements: Shutterstock: Art'nLera, grop, Marie Nimrichterova

Printed and bound in China.
004725

Table of Contents

INTRODUCTION

One Yard at a Time

Imagine you are a lawn-care specialist. You've just finished mowing your last segment of uncut grass. You stop the mower and push it under the shade of a tree in the backyard. After several hours of work, you're finally finished. You load up all of your equipment onto the bicycle trailer and pedal off to your next job. If you're looking for a way to earn money and love being outside, starting a yard-work business could be perfect for you.

A yard-work business allows you to make your own money. Money you make now can be used to buy things you want. With proper planning and saving, it can also provide you with plenty of opportunities later in life such as camps, lessons, or college. Yard work also gives you the chance to spend time outdoors. You'll get the chance to work with customers and meet new people.

CHAPTER 1
JUMPING IN

How can you get started in the yard-care business? The first step is to figure out what type of services you want to offer. This decision will depend on several factors.

What skills do you have or are willing to learn? If you already know how to mow lawns, then that would be a good service to offer. If you don't know how to mow lawns but are willing to learn, you can still add this service to your list of offerings. A family member or trusted friend can teach you.

Neighborhood Needs

If your neighborhood does not have lawns, then it doesn't make sense to provide lawn-cutting services. However, maybe your area has other types of outdoor spaces. What type of care would outdoor spaces in a city neighborhood need? A coastal neighborhood? You could water indoor plants or wash walkways. Be creative!

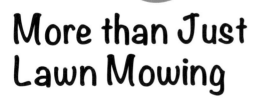

Tip

Adapt to the weather. Take advantage of the different seasons to offer your customers specialized services.

More than Just Lawn Mowing

A yard-work business can include more than just lawn mowing. Here are some other ideas:
- weeding
- tree or bush trimming
- flower or shrub planting
- garden care (vegetables and flowers)
- leaf raking and removal
- sidewalk, deck, and porch cleaning
- snow shoveling
- putting up and taking down holiday lights

Equipment

Do the adults in your life have equipment, such as lawnmowers, edgers, or hand shovels that you can borrow? Do you have your own equipment? If not, you will need to look into renting or buying equipment. Another possibility is borrowing equipment from your customer for a discount on your work fee.

Transportation

Some yard workers push their lawnmower along the sidewalk and carry their other tools. This will work if your jobs are nearby. But what if they are farther away? You'll need to have some other kind of transportation to get your equipment there. Perhaps a family member or friend could drive you to the job sites.

Tip

Keep your equipment in a secure place while you work. Equipment left out on sidewalks or driveways could be stolen. When you're not working, store equipment in a place that is well protected from weather.

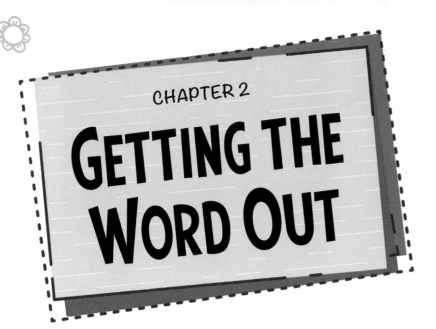

CHAPTER 2

GETTING THE WORD OUT

You've made your initial plans for your business. You know what services to offer and you've figured out what equipment to use. What's next? You'll need to find some customers. To do that, you'll need to do some **marketing**. Here are some top marketing tips.

Choose a Name

A business name is very important. You want a name that will tell your customers exactly what your business does. You also want a name that your customers will remember. Professional yard-care companies often use adjectives, **alliteration**, catchy slogans, or personal names.

Make a Logo

If you're an artist, you could make your own **logo**. Logos help people better remember a company. Think of your favorite brand name products. Are their logos recognizable? Strive to be just as memborable with your logo. For a yard-work business, you could use blades of grass, trees, flowers, or a lawnmower. Try to match your business name with your logo. For example, a logo for Emerald Lawn Care could be an illustration of a bright green lawn. Or it could be an emerald gemstone with some blades of grass. A logo isn't required, of course, but it will help your company to stand out and your customers to remember you.

Business Names Are Important!

Check out these make-believe companies and see what is good or bad about their names.

GOOD EXAMPLES	WHY IS IT GOOD?	POOR EXAMPLES	WHY IS IT POOR?
Emerald Lawn Care	Emerald is another word for "green." Everyone wants a green lawn!	Brown Lawn Care	Who wants a brown lawn? Even if your last name is Brown, avoid using it in your yard-care company's name.
Home Rangers Yard Care	A ranger is a guardian or protector. Using the word "rangers" makes people think that the company will really look after yards.	Last-Minute Yard Care	"Last minute" makes people think that you will wait until the last minute to do the work.

marketing–methods used by a company to convince people to buy its products
alliteration–the repeated use of the same sound at the beginning of words
logo–a visual symbol for a company

Advertise!

The main point of advertising is to make your business known to potential customers. Once they know who you are and what kinds of services you're offering, they'll be more likely to hire you. There are numerous ways to advertise your business. But be cautious with how much information you give out, and make sure you get permission from your parents before you start.

Posters are a great way to advertise your business. Include general information about your business, as well as your contact information on posters. Ask for permission before hanging them on job boards at your local community center, libraries, or supermarkets.

Flyers are smaller versions of posters. They contain the same important information, such as your business name and contact information. But instead of posting them at local businesses, place flyers on doorsteps in your neighborhood.

If you have your own social media account, post a picture of yourself with a lawnmower or other yard-care equipment. Write in the post that you've started a yard-work company and are looking for customers. Ask friends and family members to share your post so that it reaches more potential customers.

Business Cards

You can make simple business cards yourself, either by hand or on a computer. They don't have to be fancy. But they should be small, wallet-sized cards with your company name, logo, and contact information. If you have space, include some of the services you provide. You can also include information about your company's pricing, such as listing that you have fair or **competitive pricing**. If you decide to make your business cards on a computer, there are many free patterns online. Some online companies let you design your cards. These companies can print and mail the cards directly to you. This type of service costs money, so get an adult's permission before you order.

EMERALD
LAWN SERVICES
COMPETITIVE PRICES!
CONTACT ME AT:
EMERALDLAWN@MAIL.COM

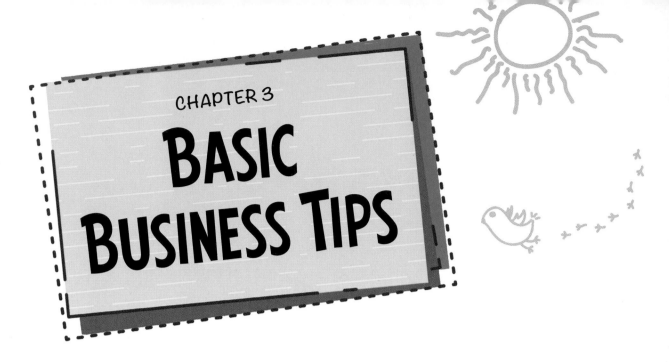

CHAPTER 3
BASIC BUSINESS TIPS

You've laid all the groundwork for the company, and you have your first job. Now the real work begins! If you want to be successful at any job, you must develop certain basic qualities. Here are a few of them.

Quality 1: Respect

Every businessperson must show kindness and respect to his or her customers. This is absolutely necessary for the success of a business. If you don't listen to customer concerns or treat them rudely, chances are they won't hire you anymore. Of course, there might be a time when a customer is rude to you. You can't control what others will do, but you can control your response. If a customer is rude, be as nice as possible, and try to resolve the problem. If this doesn't change the customer's attitude, then perhaps it's time to stop working with him or her. But for the sake of your business reputation, never be rude back!

Another way to show respect is to use "Mr." or "Ms." along with the customer's last name. Once jobs are complete, it's also polite to shake customers' hands and thank them for the opportunity of doing business.

Quality 2: Good Impressions

There are many ways to make a good impression. First, always use polite language. Being on time for each of your jobs makes a good impression. It shows customers that you are dependable and value their time and schedule.

Since this is a yard-work business, you won't need to choose clothes that are too dressy, but be sure you are appropriately dressed. Wear clean and tidy clothing.

Quality 3: Communication Skills

Business owners must be able to talk to their employees and their customers. Some people have natural communication abilities. They just seem to be able to talk to anyone about anything. Even if communication isn't one of your strengths, you can work on improving it.

If you're shy, think about what you will say ahead of time. Come up with a script and practice it. Make sure in your script you introduce yourself and state your purpose. Sometimes the script will vary in different situations. Pretend a friend, family member, or even your pet is a potential customer, and practice your script.

Quality 4: High-Quality Work

The best way to get more customers is to do your current jobs as well as you can. The work you do on the job is more effective than any other form of advertising. As your reputation grows, so will your business.

Tip

After you have completed your work, always ask your customers if there is anything else you can help them with. You never know when they might have another job for you to do, either that day or on a return visit.

Motivation Matters

Sometimes the motivation to do high-quality work might not be there. Maybe you're having a bad day, or maybe you feel like you have too much to do. Don't sweat! Here are three tips to help get you through even your worst slumps.

1. Make small, specific goals. If you have a lot to do at a job, it's easy to get overwhelmed. Break up the work into bits and pieces, and only concentrate on one piece at a time. Is the yard really big? Break it into fourths and do one quarter at a time. Before you know it, you'll be done!

2. Be your own cheerleader. It's important to encourage yourself and be positive. Cut back on negative thoughts. So "I don't want to do this today," turns into, "My clients really appreciate my work."

3. Remember why you started. When all you want to do is give up and quit, remember why you decided to start your business. Keep that reason alive and let it motivate you to be the best you can be.

CHAPTER 4

MONEY MANAGEMENT

Good business people know how to manage their money. This is true no matter the age of the business owner. You can probably spend some of your earnings on fun things such as video games. But don't forget that you might need to invest money back into the business by buying equipment and fuel. A business will not grow unless **profits** are spent wisely.

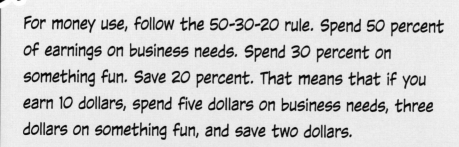

Tip

For money use, follow the 50-30-20 rule. Spend 50 percent of earnings on business needs. Spend 30 percent on something fun. Save 20 percent. That means that if you earn 10 dollars, spend five dollars on business needs, three dollars on something fun, and save two dollars.

Opening a Bank Account

Since you'll be earning money from your yard-care business, you may want to set up a bank account. To do so, a parent or guardian will most likely need to be with you.

As a young person, you'll most likely open a savings account. This is a special account that focuses on saving and accumulating money for long-term purposes.

The bank uses your money to loan to others, and then pays you **interest**. The amount of money you'll make from interest will be small, but in a business, every penny earned helps.

profit—the amount of money left after all the costs of running a business have been subtracted
interest—the cost of borrowing money; reward for saving money

Money Plans

All business owners should make a **budget**. This will help the business stay on track and grow. There are several things to consider when creating a yard-work business budget. Here are a few things to think about.

How much gasoline will you need for your upcoming jobs? Remember that gasoline is something that varies in price every week. Because of its unpredictable nature, plan for the worst. Look at how expensive gas has been in your area for the last few weeks. Find the highest price and assume gas will cost that much. Keep track of how much grass you can mow with one tank of gas. You could write this information down in a small notebook. This will help you figure out how much gas you will need per job. Put aside enough gas money for the amount of jobs you have.

Tip

Remember, in addition to gasoline you might also need oil and other fuels for the equipment. Keep this in mind and include any extra materials in your budget.

Building Your Budget

Building a budget doesn't have to be complicated. In many cases, free templates found online will work for your growing business. Most budgets are broken into monthly costs. Don't forget these three important parts to your budget.

1. **Income.** How much money do you make each month? This will depend on how many regular customers you have. Make sure you update this total as you add more customers or services. Income minus costs determines how much profit you will make each month.

2. **Fixed costs.** These are expenses that are consistent month to month. Are you making payments on a new lawnmower? This type of payment will be the same each month, and should be accounted for in your budget.

3. **Variable costs.** These are consistent expenses that can change month to month. Variable costs mostly depend on how much activity and product your business puts out. For example, how much money you spend on gas changes depending on how many times you use your lawnmower. Try to include an average amount of each variable cost to your budget.

budget—a plan for spending and saving money

income—the total amount of money a person makes or receives

fixed cost—an expense that does not change over time

variable cost—an expense that can change

23

Do you need to save for any new equipment? Do you want to purchase new equipment in five months? Three? Find out how much the equipment costs. Then figure out how much money you need to put aside every month to save for it. If you are using older equipment, it could break down. Keep money in your bank account to cover the cost of any emergency repairs.

Are there things you need to buy to offer new services? Adding new services to your business will help your business grow. However, you can't offer snow removal if you don't own a snow shovel. Think ahead and decide what goals you have for your business. Then decide how you will save money in your budget so you can accomplish those goals.

Tip
Have a family member or trusted adult help you figure out your budget and finances. He or she may have years of experience and might have some really valuable advice to give.

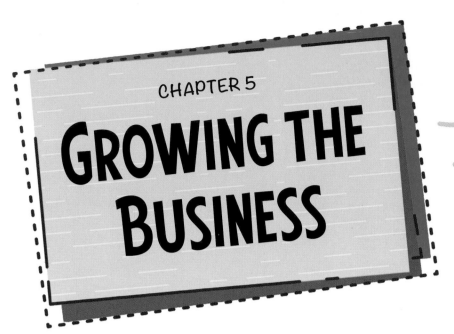

CHAPTER 5

GROWING THE BUSINESS

In the beginning, perhaps you started your yard-work business to have a little extra money for fun things. However, things may end up going better than you thought. If that is the case, consider ways to expand your business.

Getting More Work

To grow your business and profits, simply find more customers. If you can travel further away, start adding more neighborhoods to your business range.

Adding Services

Another way to grow is by offering additional services that will help attract more customers. Try to pick up work in more than just one season. Offer leaf collection in the fall, snow removal in the winter, and spring cleaning in the spring.

Hiring Help

Once you have more work than you can handle yourself, you may need to hire employees. In many cases, siblings or friends will work. Just make sure you treat them as fairly as you would your customers, and pay them for their help. Add their wages as a fixed cost into your budget.

Your business could grow from a one-person operation to a multi-employee company. Just remember to dream big, work hard, and ask for advice from experts along the way. If you do, you can make your business extraordinary!

GLOSSARY

alliteration (uh-lit-uh-RAY-shuhn)—the repeated use of the same sound at the beginning of words

budget (BUH-juht)—a plan for spending and saving money

competitive price (kuhm-PET-uh-tiv PRISSE)—the cost of a product or service that is as low as other businesses

fixed cost (FIKSD KAWST)—an expense that does not change over time

income (IN-kuhm)—the total amount of money a person makes or receives

interest (IN-trist)—the cost of borrowing money; reward for saving money

logo (LOH-goh)—a visual symbol for a company

marketing (MAR-ket-ing)—methods used by a company to convince people to buy its products

profit (PROF-it)—the amount of money left after all the costs of running a business have been subtracted

variable cost (VAIR-ee-uh-buhl KAHST)—an expense that can change

READ MORE

Braun, Eric and Sandy Donovan. *The Survival Guide for Money Smarts: Earn, Save, Spend, Give.* Minneapolis: Free Spirit Publishing, 2016.

Kopp, Megan. *Maker Projects for Kids Who Love Greening Up Spaces.* Be a Maker! New York: Crabtree Publishing, 2017.

McGuire, Kara. *All About the Green: The Teens' Guide to Finding Work and Making Money.* Financial Literacy for Teens. North Mankato, Minn.: Capstone Publishing, 2015.

INTERNET SITES

FactHound offers a safe, fun way to find Internet sites related to this book. All of the sites on FactHound have been researched by our staff.

Here's all you do:
Visit *www.facthound.com*

Type in this code: 9781515766926

Check out projects, games and lots more at
www.capstonekids.com

INDEX